MAGIC TRICKS
WITH
COINS,
CARDS,
AND
EVERYDAY
OBJECTS

Quarto is the authority on a wide range of topics.

Quarto educates, entertains and enriches the lives of our readers—enthusiasts and lovers of hands-on living.

www.quartoknows.com

Photographer: Michael Wicks
Designer: Amy McSimpson, Hollow Pond
Project Designer: Victoria Kimonidou
Cover Designer: Mike Henson
Editor: Clare Hibbert, Hollow Pond
Project Editor: Joanna McInerney

First published in the US in 2017 by
QEB Publishing
Part of The Quarto Group
6 Orchard, lake Forest, CA 92630

A catalog record for this book is available from the Library of Congress.

ISBN 978 1 68297 151 2

9 8 7 6 5 4 3

Manufactured in in Guangdong, China CC102017

KEY

★ REALLY EASY
★★ PRETTY EASY
★★★ AVERAGE DIFFICULTY
★★★★ PRETTY HARD
★★★★★ REALLY HARD

CONTENTS

FOREWORD

The first time I saw a really good magic trick, I thought... "WOW! I need to learn how to do that!" Now, I can't remember a time when I didn't do magic.

I fell in love with magic when I was really young, and I haven't stopped learning tricks since. The truth is I get such a rush from the moment I absolutely astound someone with a cool trick. The feeling you get when you see your audience gasp and marvel at an effect is addictive and I love it. I'm sure you will too.

The tricks you will learn in this book will turn you from *regular you* into *super magic you*. It is the book I wish I had when I first started to learn magic. I've chosen the tricks that will truly amaze your friends and family. Every single trick will impress.

Over the last decade, magic has changed and evolved. Odd-looking props have been thrown out of the window—audiences don't trust them and suspect that they have been tampered with (and they

OVER TO YOU!

usually have been!). That's why the tricks in this book use everyday objects. There is nothing more magical than taking an ordinary object and doing something extraordinary with it. Your audience will be surprised and even more amazed because they didn't know that this pen or that coin had such magical properties. They assume they are just boring everday objects, and as magicians we can use that to our advantage!

Cool characters like Tony Slydini, Fred Kaps, and Channing Pollock had such style. They pushed the boundaries of what defined "magic" and have all left the art in a better place than they found it. That's my goal and part of the reason I wrote this book—to give a new generation of young magicians the skills and tricks to go out there and become legends.

Technology is developing at an increasingly fast rate. New gadgets are always being released that on the surface seem pretty magical. Yet, a simple magic trick still has its place. It reminds people that there are still things out there to be discovered, still mysteries to be solved, and that there are still things that prompt wonder and awe. Try to remember that notion when performing the tricks in this book.

Take these tricks and make them magic!

Jake Banfield

INTRODUCTION

Most people love to see magic. I'm sharing these tricks with you because I want you to be able to ASTONISH your audiences by showing them something amazing.

JAKE'S MAGIC RULES

1 Never reveal the secret to a trick. People will ask how you did it, but they don't really want to know. Seeing and experiencing good magic is a far better feeling than knowing how something is done.

2 Make sure you understand, practice, and master each trick before you perform it. You want each trick to work so well that no one can tell how it's done. Seeing you make a blunder will destroy your audience's bafflement and wonder.

3 Last but not least, enjoy yourself! Doing tricks brought me out of my shell and has given me the confidence to talk to anyone. I hope the everyday magic in this book does the same for you.

TIP
The mark of a true magician is being ready for anything.

TRIOS OF TRICKS

Pick tricks that fit into groups of three: an opener, a middle, and a closing trick. The opener should be quick and amazing. The middle trick can be slightly longer now that you've grabbed your audience's attention. Your final trick should be the best of them all and leave your audience wanting more.

Here are three trios to try:

MIND READING

Book Test (p104)
Lottery Prediction (p96)
Phone Prediction Trick (p22)

COMBINATION SET

Coin Through Hand (p40)
The Vanishing Bottle (p90)
Phone Prediction Trick (p22)

CARD TRICKS

Card in Mouth (p30)
Si Stebbins' Stack (p36)
Sneaky Card Swap (p18)

ENJOY!

REHEARSALS AND PRACTICE

The only way to become a master magician is to practice, practice, **PRACTICE!** Put in the hours when you're learning a new trick and remember to revisit your old tricks regularly so you don't become rusty.

1 Learn new sleights slowly, taking time to make sure your hands are in the correct positions. It's no good practicing for hours if what you're learning isn't right.

2 Mimic natural mannerisms. When you do a **double lift**, make it look exactly the same as when you turn over only the top card of the deck.

TIP

If you get stuck learning a new sleight, take a break. Come back to it a few hours or even a few days later.

3 If the sleight doesn't look natural, train your mannerisms to match the sleight. Look as relaxed as you can—even when a position's a bit awkward.

CRACK!

4 If you practice in front of a mirror, remember that you're only seeing the trick from one angle.

5 Stretch your hands before you begin. With practice, they'll get used to moving in new ways and the sleight of hand will become second nature.

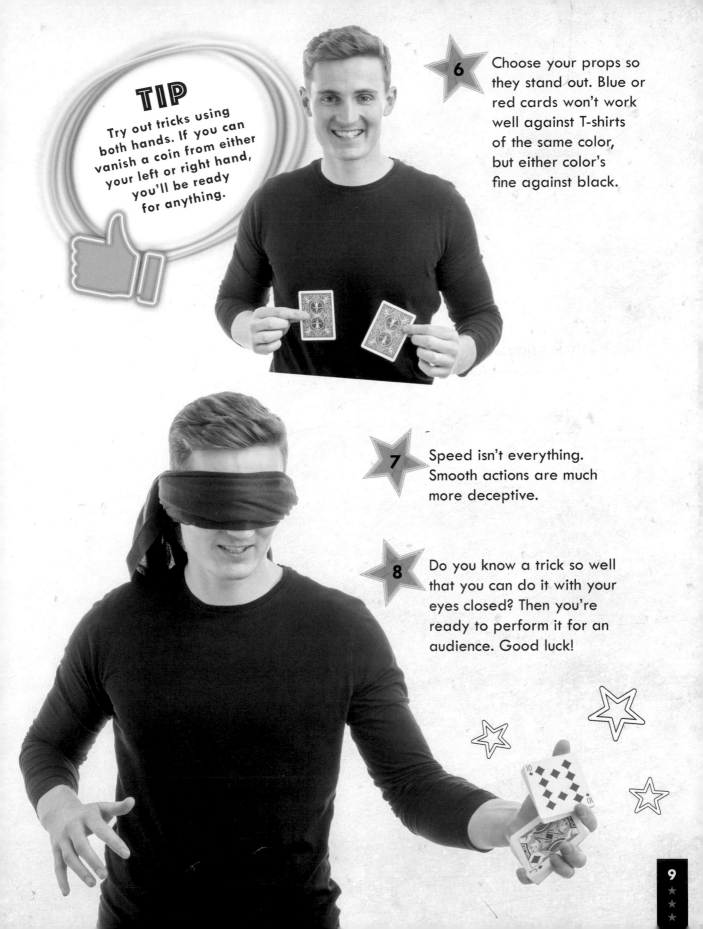

6 Choose your props so they stand out. Blue or red cards won't work well against T-shirts of the same color, but either color's fine against black.

7 Speed isn't everything. Smooth actions are much more deceptive.

8 Do you know a trick so well that you can do it with your eyes closed? Then you're ready to perform it for an audience. Good luck!

STYLE AND PERFORMANCE

There are many ways of performing magic. Developing your own STYLE takes time. Experiment with different tricks and approaches, from funny or clumsy to serious and mysterious.

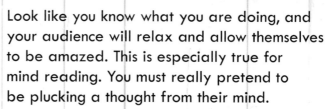

PERFORMANCE TIPS

1 Loosen your face muscles before you go on stage. It will make you more relaxed—and make your voice naturally louder too.

2 Look like you know what you are doing, and your audience will relax and allow themselves to be amazed. This is especially true for mind reading. You must really pretend to be plucking a thought from their mind.

3 When the magic moment happens, it is okay for you to react to the magic too. This gives the audience a signal that it is okay for them to be amazed.

4 Your audience will follow your eyes when you perform a trick and look where you look. Try looking into your audience's eyes during a secret move—they'll look at your face, not your hands.

WHAT TO WEAR

Clothes are a part of your act. They affect how people look at you and your magic.

Just wear your normal clothes...

...or smarten up in a jacket.

Go for a quirky bow tie...

...or try a saucy hat.

Just find a style that suits you.

CARD TRICK BASICS

Knowledge of these few basic card trick principles will give you the foundation to do all the card magic in this book and MORE. Learn to handle cards the right way from the start.

SPECIAL HOLDS

BIDDLE GRIP

Hold the card or cards from the top. Grip one short end with your middle, ring, and little fingers and the other with your thumb. Bend your index finger and gently rest it on the top of the card or cards.

MECHANIC'S GRIP

Hold the card or cards from the bottom. Grip one long end with your middle, ring, and little fingers and rest the other against the base of your thumb. Use your index finger to hold the short end farthest away from you.

FINGER BREAK

Use your little finger to keep a gap in the deck of cards, to mark the position of a particular card. So long as you hold the cards at an angle, the gap can be quite large and the audience won't see it.

YOU'RE IN CONTROL

Force card

HINDU FORCE

Hold the deck in biddle grip with the **force** card at the bottom. Pull cards from the top of the deck into your other hand until your volunteer calls "Stop!" Then revolve the cards that are left to show them the bottom card (your force card).

TOP CARD CONTROL

Cut the cards, holding the top half in biddle grip and the bottom half in mechanic's grip. Ask your volunteer to place their chosen card on the lower half. When you rejoin the two halves, keep a finger break between them.

Chosen card is on top of bottom half

Pick up the top half in a biddle grip and revolve both halves so they are face up. **Shuffle** off a few cards from the face of the upper half onto the lower half, then place the rest of the upper half onto the face of the lower half. Your force card is at the top.

Chosen card here will end up at the top

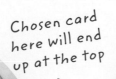

Pick a card! Any card!

SMELL YOUR CARD

Can you pick out a card just by giving it a sniff? Impress your audience with your INCREDIBLE sense of smell.

YOU WILL NEED:
- one deck of cards
- a table

TIP
This trick uses the **KEY CARD PRINCIPLE**. Don't be spotted peeking at the bottom card.

1 Ask your volunteer to **shuffle** the cards. As they give you the deck back, glimpse the bottom card and remember it. This will be your key card.

2 Fan the cards face down. Ask the volunteer to choose one and remember it.

3 Cut a portion from the top of the deck and place on the table. Repeat until the volunteer says "Stop!" Ask them to return the chosen card to the pile. Place the rest of the deck directly on top of this pile.

Now the volunteer's card is next to your key card in the pack.

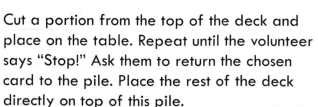

4 Pretend to shuffle the cards. Slide off about half of the cards and dump the rest on top of these. Repeat a few times to create the illusion of a thorough shuffle.

S-S-N-I-I-F-F-F-F!

5 Now for the fun part—sniffing your volunteer! This has nothing to do with how you find the chosen card, but it entertains the audience—and throws them off the scent of how you do the trick.

6 Fan the cards so they face you. Pretend to sniff them but actually look for your key card. The card below that will be your volunteer's chosen card.

Who NOSE how you did it?!

7 Nose the card up out of the deck...

8 ...and reveal it to the volunteer.

UPSIDE-DOWN CARD

In this simple trick, the volunteer's chosen card **MAGICALLY** appears in the center of the deck —but mysteriously the wrong way up.

YOU WILL NEED:
• one deck of cards

1 Fan the deck and ask the volunteer to choose a card. Before they look at it, tell them that you will turn around so you cannot get a glimpse of the card.

2 With your back to the volunteer, turn the deck face up and the new top card face down. Hold in **mechanic's grip**.

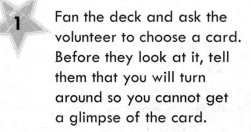

magician's view

TIP
Make sure you don't move the top card and accidentally reveal which way up the deck is.

3 Turn back to face the volunteer and ask them to slide their card face down into the pack wherever they like. The volunteer doesn't know they're placing their card face down in a secretly face-up deck.

4 Say you'll find the card behind your back in less than three seconds. When the cards are behind you, quickly turn the top card face up again.

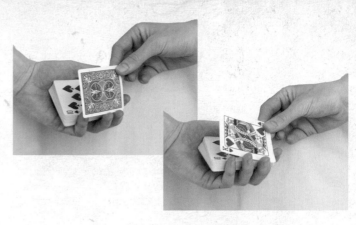

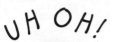

5 Bring the cards back out. Whatever the card on top is, ask the volunteer if this is their card. Of course it isn't, so it will look like the trick has gone wrong.

This is what's known as a SUCKER TRICK—one where you make the audience think it's gone wrong, when actually it will work out in the end.

6 Tell your volunteer not to worry—with a little bit of magic you can make all the cards turn face up. Snap your fingers, wave over the deck, and fan the cards. One will be face down. Ask the volunteer to pull it from the fan to reveal...their CHOSEN CARD.

SNEAKY CARD SWAP

This trick uses two really useful card magic sleights: a top card control and a double lift. Distract your audience with CHITCHAT so they don't look too closely at your hands.

YOU WILL NEED:
• one deck of cards

1 Ask a volunteer to pick a card from the fanned deck and remember it. Spread the cards again and ask the volunteer to return their card to the bottom half.

2

magician's view

As you replace the top cards, keep a little **finger break** between the two halves...but don't let anyone see.

3 **Cut** off the top quarter of the cards and place them down. Then cut off all the cards above the little finger break and place on top of the pile.

4 Drop the remaining half onto the pile. The chosen card is at the top.

5 Hold the deck in **mechanic's grip** in your left hand. Use the side of your right first finger to pull up the top card and, secretly, the fingertip to pull up the second. Pinch both cards as one and turn them over.

This is a **double lift** —you seemed to lift one card, but it was two.

TIP
Keep both cards square so they look like one.

6 Use your left first finger to create a break between the turned-over pair—the double—and the rest of the deck. Ask the volunteer if this is their card. Then turn the double face down.

UH OH!

7 Take only the top card this time and place it face down on the volunteer's palm.

ALAKAZAM!

8 Wave your hand over the volunteer's. Amazing! The card has changed into the chosen one.

POP-UP CARD

Magicians call this famous trick the Ambitious Card Trick. A member of the audience chooses a card and pushes it into the middle of the pack. AMAZINGLY, the card jumps to the top of the deck at the magician's command—not once, but twice.

1 Ask the volunteer to pick a card from the deck and draw or write on it. Meanwhile, secretly turn the top two cards face up and keep a break under them.

2 Place the chosen card face up on the face-up two cards, keeping the **finger break**.

TIP
Keep the deck toward you, being careful not to reveal the face-up cards.

3 Turn over all three cards as one...

4 ...then place the top card, which the audience thinks is the chosen one, in the middle of the deck.

5 The bottom card isn't theirs...

6 ...and neither is the top one! Get a little finger break under the second card as you replace the top one.

7 Do a **double lift**—now the top card IS the chosen one.

8 Turn the double down, then drop the top card onto the table. Cascade the other cards on top until only one is left...the chosen card.

NOW, HOW DID THAT GET THERE?

PHONE PREDICTION TRICK

This trick uses the Hindu force. Like any force, it'll trick your audience into believing they actively chose the card—and leave them BAFFLED about how you managed to predict it ahead of the trick.

YOU WILL NEED:
- one deck of cards
- a cell phone

You will choose the Seven of Hearts.

1 Place the **force** card at the bottom of the deck. Text its name to your volunteer—but don't let them read the message yet.

2 Hold the deck in **biddle grip** with the right hand, and pull off cards a few at a time from the top using your left hand. Ask your volunteer to call "Stop!"

magician's view

TIP
NEVER look at your hands when you're performing secret sleights.

3 Stop shuffling and rotate the right-hand pile to face them, revealing your force card (which was at the bottom). Ask them to remember their card.

4 Show the volunteer all the cards now if you like, so they know they're all different.

5 *Now* your volunteer can read their text message. It's magic!

23

DOUBLE-STUCK CARD PREDICTION

Double-sided tape is the magician's friend. With a little SNEAKY pre-show preparation, it'll make your volunteer's chosen card the only blue one in a pack of red cards.

TIP
FACE CARDS work best for this trick.

YOU WILL NEED:
- one deck of red-backed cards
- one deck of blue-backed cards
- double-sided tape • scissors

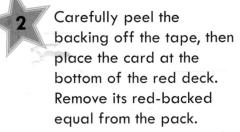

1 Choose a blue playing card. Stick some double-sided tape on its face.

The chance of them naming the same card you chose is very small—just one in 52.

2 Carefully peel the backing off the tape, then place the card at the bottom of the red deck. Remove its red-backed equal from the pack.

3 For the trick, ask a volunteer to name a card.

4a If they say the card you have already prepared —in this case, the Queen of Spades—you have a miracle! Show them that it's the only blue card in the deck. Trick done. Handled!

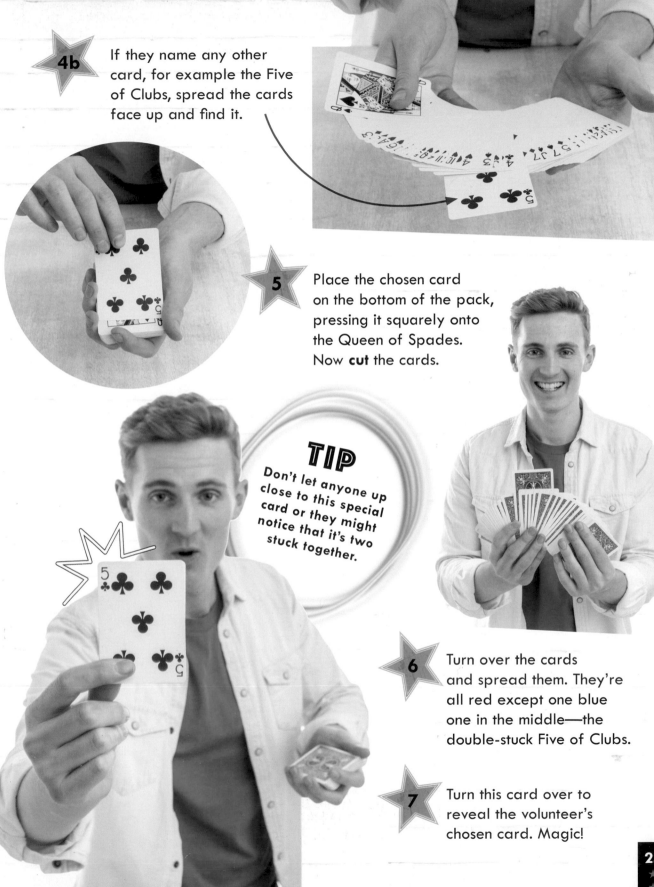

4b If they name any other card, for example the Five of Clubs, spread the cards face up and find it.

5 Place the chosen card on the bottom of the pack, pressing it squarely onto the Queen of Spades. Now **cut** the cards.

TIP
Don't let anyone up close to this special card or they might notice that it's two stuck together.

6 Turn over the cards and spread them. They're all red except one blue one in the middle—the double-stuck Five of Clubs.

7 Turn this card over to reveal the volunteer's chosen card. Magic!

DO AS I DO

In this clever trick, you and your volunteer each have your own deck of cards that you pick a card from. What are the chances you both choose the same card? Pretty high when there's MAGIC involved!

YOU WILL NEED:
• two decks of cards

Your volunteer shuffles this deck...

...and you shuffle this one.

1 Give one deck to your volunteer and each **shuffle** your deck. Then swap decks. As you hand over yours, glimpse the bottom card—your **key card**.

2 Ask the volunteer to copy your moves. Spread the face-down deck and choose a card at random. Ask the volunteer to do the same and remember their card. Place both selected cards to one side.

TIP
Pretend to memorize your own card, but you won't actually need it!

You

Your volunteer

3 **Cut** a portion of cards from the top of your deck and put them on the table. Cut another portion and place on the tabled pile.

Selected cards

4 Place your chosen card on the tabled pile...

5 ...and drop the rest of the deck on top. Now your key card is on top of the volunteer's chosen card.

TIP
You appear to be looking for YOUR chosen card but really you are finding the volunteer's.

6 Swap decks again. Tell your volunteer to find their chosen card in the deck they are holding.

7 Meanwhile, spread the deck they gave you and locate your key card. The card below it is the volunteer's chosen card.

1... 2... 3... TA-DAH!

A BAFFLING SPELL

Turn your volunteer into a magician for this amazing card trick. With some CRAFTY math, you can make magic happen in your volunteer's own hands—and they won't have a clue how.

YOU WILL NEED:

- nine random playing cards

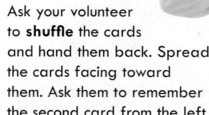

Remember this one.

1 Ask your volunteer to **shuffle** the cards and hand them back. Spread the cards facing toward them. Ask them to remember the second card from the left.

2 Give the volunteer the cards. Ask them to spell out their name, placing one card on the table for every letter.

3 Now ask them to drop the rest of the cards on top.

4 Now ask the volunteer to spell the word "LOVES," one card for each letter, and drop the rest on top.

TIP

Each word or name must be more than two letters long but less than nine letters.

5 Lastly ask them to spell the name of someone or something that they love. It might be "MOM" or even "PIZZA." Ask them to drop the other cards on top again.

This trick is so good it can even be done over the phone! You don't need to be with the volunteer so long as they follow your instructions!

6 The chosen card will ALWAYS be third from the bottom. Ask the volunteer to deal the cards slowly onto the table. Tell them to stop just before the seventh card and say you sense it's their chosen one.

CARD IN MOUTH

Fake "mistakes" in a trick are a surefire way to raise laughs. This classic involves sleight of MOUTH as well as sleight of hand and it finishes on the tip of your tongue!

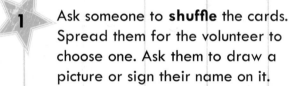
YOU WILL NEED:
• one deck of cards • a pen

1 Ask someone to **shuffle** the cards. Spread them for the volunteer to choose one. Ask them to draw a picture or sign their name on it.

2 Use **top card control** to bring the card to the top of the deck. Say you'll find their card behind your back without looking.

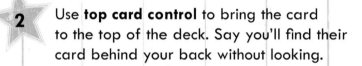

TIP
See page 13 for more about top card control.

3 Behind your back, hold the deck in **biddle grip,** with your right thumb poking farther than normal. Use your left-hand fingers to slide the chosen card and fold it in half.

4 Fold the card around your right thumb. Squeeze the creases nice and sharp.

5 Keep the folded card on top of the deck. Pull out any card you like with your right hand and hold it face down.

6 Now bring both hands in front of you. Turn over the card in your right hand with a flourish. But of course, it's not the card.

TA-DAH!

7 Bring the deck to your mouth, bite it and, as you do, slide the folded card into your mouth with your thumb. Then spread the cards and pull a random card from the center.

magician's view

8 Move away your hands. Was this their card?

UH OH!

9 Hang your head in shame for a moment, then begin to cough. Push the card from your mouth...and it's the chosen card! Incredible!

CARD IN WALLET

In this trick, you put two Aces into the volunteer's wallet or purse. What they don't realize, until the REVEAL, is that you've hidden their chosen card between the Aces too.

YOU WILL NEED:
- one deck of cards • a pen
- a wallet or purse

1 Ask someone to **shuffle** the cards. Spread them for the volunteer to choose one. Ask them to draw a picture or sign their name on it. Take the card and use **top card control** to bring it to the top of the deck.

2 Fan the cards to remove the two red Aces.

magician's view

3 With your left hand, push up the top card to get a litle **finger break** under it.

4 Pop the Aces on top of the deck, then pick up the three cards above the break in **biddle grip**. Slide the top Ace onto the deck with your left thumb.

5 Let the other Ace (with the chosen card underneath) slide on top. Keep a finger break below the three cards.

6 Ask the volunteer for their wallet and carefully slide the Aces into it.

TIP
Make sure that no one spots the chosen card sandwiched between the Aces.

TIP
Have a fun bet with your volunteer. Say if you can find their card in less than three seconds, then you get to keep EVERYTHING in their wallet!

7 Hand the deck to the volunteer and ask them to shuffle the cards.

8 Ask the volunteer to turn over the top card...but it's not theirs. Doh!

HANG ON A MINUTE... WHAT'S THAT EXTRA CARD?

9 Never mind. Open their wallet and spread the Aces (or ask them to do this).

CARD IN ORANGE

This FRUITY trick takes some super-secret preparation. The audience watches as a chosen card disappears into thin air—and reappears inside an orange. Delicious!

calyx

1 Take the calyx off the orange and put it to one side. Push the pencil into the orange (but not all the way through).

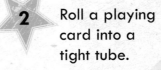

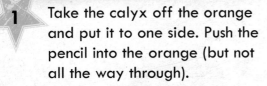

2 Roll a playing card into a tight tube.

Remember this card

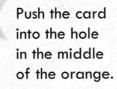

3 Push the card into the hole in the middle of the orange.

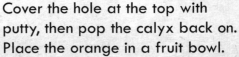

4 Cover the hole at the top with putty, then pop the calyx back on. Place the orange in a fruit bowl.

5 From the second deck, take a duplicate of the card hidden in the orange. Stick a square of double-sided tape on its face, then place on the bottom of the original deck.

NOW FOR THE TRICK!

6 Force the prepared card on your audience using the **Hindu force**. Show the card to the audience, then square the pack back up. The card will stick to the one below it.

7 Spread the cards face up. The chosen card has disappeared.

TIP
Cut open the orange if you prefer—just be careful not to cut your fingers or the card.

8 Take the secretly prepared orange and peel it. There's a card inside...

9 ...not just any card—THEIR card!

SI STEBBINS' STACK

Named after a 19th-century American magician, the Si Stebbins' Stack is a pack of cards in a special order. Knowing the order makes guessing cards EASY —but to any outsider, the pack looks totally ordinary.

YOU WILL NEED:
• one deck of cards

TIP

To remember the order of the suits, think of the word **CHaSeD** (Clubs, Hearts, Spades, Diamonds). Diamonds goes back to Clubs.

1 First prepare your cards. To put them in the right order, follow this table.

2 Using this stack, you can always tell what the next card in the deck will be— you simply add 3 to the value of the card you see and move to the next suit.

TIP

Numbers go "round the clock" —so adding 3 to the Jack takes you to the Ace.

CLUBS	HEARTS	SPADES	DIAMONDS
2	5	8	JACK
ACE	4	7	10
KING	3	6	9
QUEEN	2	5	8
JACK	ACE	4	7
10	KING	3	6
9	QUEEN	2	5
8	JACK	ACE	4
7	10	KING	3
6	9	QUEEN	2
5	8	JACK	ACE
4	7	10	KING
3	6	9	QUEEN

The card above the Jack of Diamonds will be the Ace of Clubs.

The card above the Three of Diamonds will be the Six of Clubs.

USING THE STACK

TIP
Don't worry! Cutting the cards won't affect the order of the stack!

1 Give the deck to a volunteer and ask them to look through and make sure they're not marked or in any particular order (even though they are).

2 Tell them to hold the deck behind their back and **cut** the cards. They can do this a few times until they are happy.

3 Now tell your volunteer to take off the top card without looking at it and place it into a pocket.

4 Take back the deck to put the cards away. As you do so, secretly glimpse the bottom card. Add on 3 and change to the next suit and you'll know the exact identity of the mystery card in the volunteer's pocket. Genius!

COIN TRICK BASICS

Become a master of coin magic and you will become a master of sleight of hand. The sleights, palms, and techniques in this chapter will help with ALL your other magic too.

VANISHING METHODS

FRENCH DROP

1 Hold the coin between your left first two fingers and thumb. Move your right hand across it, with your thumb going behind the coin.

2 Pretend to take the coin with your right hand, but actually drop it down into **finger palm** in the left hand.

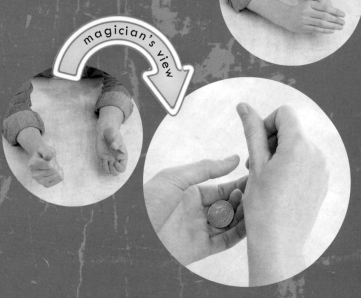

magician's view

3 Turn the left hand palm down, hiding the coin, and the right hand palm up.

ALL THREE VANISHING METHODS LEAD TO THE SAME FINALE: YOU SLOWLY OPEN YOUR RIGHT HAND...

...AND THE COIN'S GONE!

FALSE TRANSFER

1 Rest the coin at the base of the fingers of your open left hand.

2 Pretend to toss the coin into your right hand, but actually curl your left-hand fingers around it and hold in finger palm. Close your right fist around the imaginary coin.

magician's view

magician's view

...AND THE COIN'S GONE!

...AND THE COIN'S GONE!

FAKE TAKE

1 Balance the coin on the second finger of your open left hand, with the finger raised a little.

2 Move your right hand across and pretend to pick up the coin. But actually knock the coin so it falls into finger palm.

COIN REPRODUCTION

1 With a coin concealed in finger palm, turn your hand palm down.

2 Extend your fingers and slide the coin along them using your thumb.

3 Just as the coin comes into view, tilt your hand to show off the coin at your fingertips.

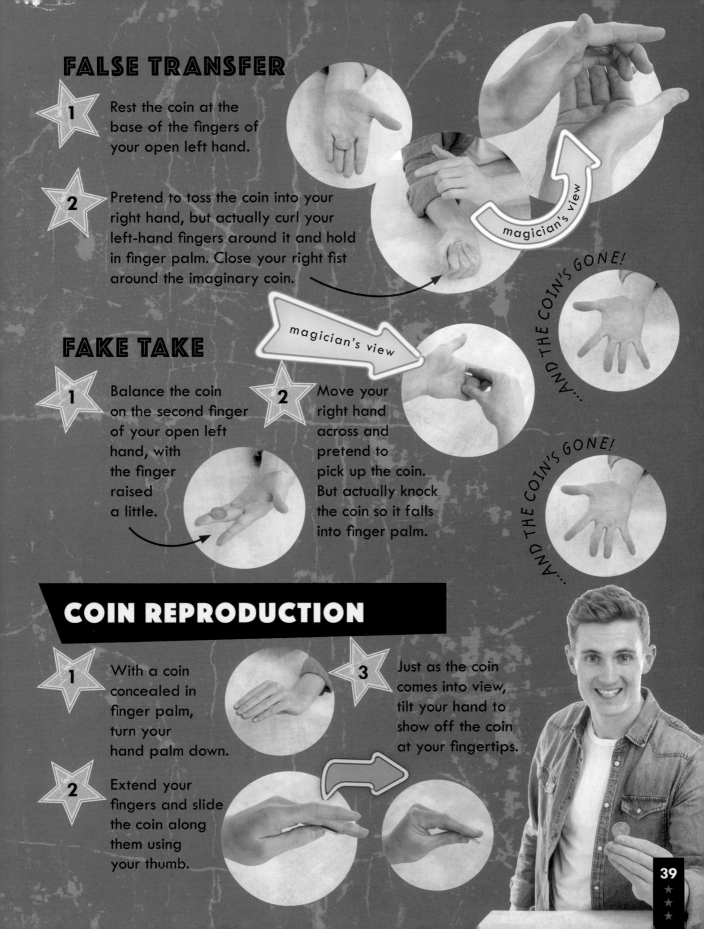

COIN T OUG AND

This handy trick is sure to impress. Tell your volunteer that you're going to test their reactions—then see their reaction when you MAGICALLY melt a coin through their fist.

YOU WILL NEED:
- four coins

TIP

Drop the first three coins gently from your right-hand fingers. Tip the last coin onto the rest with your left hand.

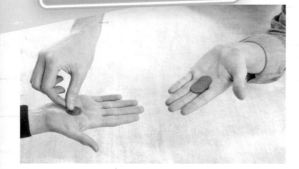

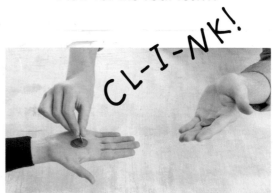

1 Ask the volunteer to hold out their right hand. Show them four coins in your left hand. Explain that you'll count the coins into their hand...

2 ...and they must close their fist tightly after you drop in the last coin. Say: "Good job! Now for the real test..."

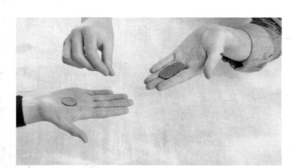

CL-I-NK!

3 Repeat the process with the first two coins, dropping them onto the volunteer's palm from your right hand.

4 Tap the third coin onto the first two, but don't actually let go of it.

5 Start to tip the fourth coin from your left hand on top of the first two. At the same time, move your right hand, which is still holding the third coin, directly below the volunteer's hand —where they cannot see it.

6 Your volunteer should close their fist, unaware they are holding only three coins. Your right hand is holding the other coin behind their hand.

The volunteer is usually so convinced they were holding **FOUR** coins that they think you used an extra coin. When they open their hand and see only **THREE** coins, they really are baffled.

7 Slowly rub the back of their hand and then pretend to pull the coin through it. Magic!

SPELLBOUND COINS

This coin trick is SUPER cool—but with three sleight-of-hands, it takes practice to carry it off perfectly.

YOU WILL NEED:
• two different coins
(e.g. a penny and a quarter)

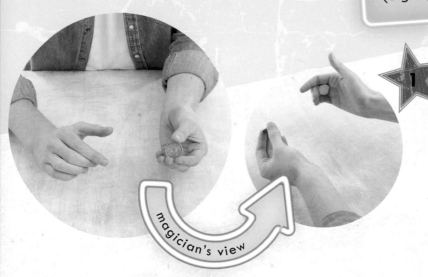

magician's view

1 Start with a penny in **French drop** position in your left hand and a quarter **finger-palmed** in the right hand.

SWAP 1! BOOM!

magician's view

2 Move your right-hand fingers to cover the penny. Secretly take it between your thumb and the base of your first finger. This is a **thumb palm**.

3 Put the quarter in French drop display position as you move your hand away.

4 Move the right hand back over the quarter. Use your thumb to knock the quarter into finger palm in the left hand and take the penny from thumb palm back into French drop display.

SWAP 2! BOOM! BOOM!

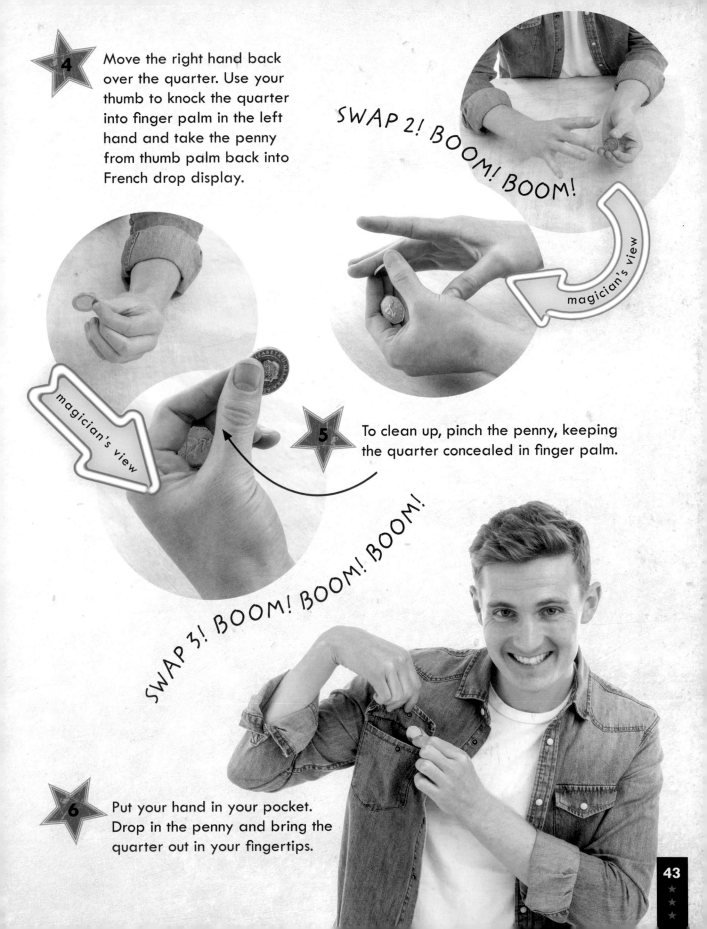

magician's view

magician's view

5 To clean up, pinch the penny, keeping the quarter concealed in finger palm.

SWAP 3! BOOM! BOOM! BOOM!

6 Put your hand in your pocket. Drop in the penny and bring the quarter out in your fingertips.

15

STUCK ON VANISH

Once you've mastered this trick, you can use it to make ANY small object disappear, not just a coin.

YOU WILL NEED:
• one coin • reusable adhesive putty

1 Stick the coin to the back of your right hand with putty. Keep this hand palm up so the coin cannot be seen.

The audience follow your eyes and look where YOU look.

2 Flip an imaginary coin from your left hand to the back of your right hand. As you go to catch it, hide the stuck-on coin from your audience with your fingers.

P-A-T!

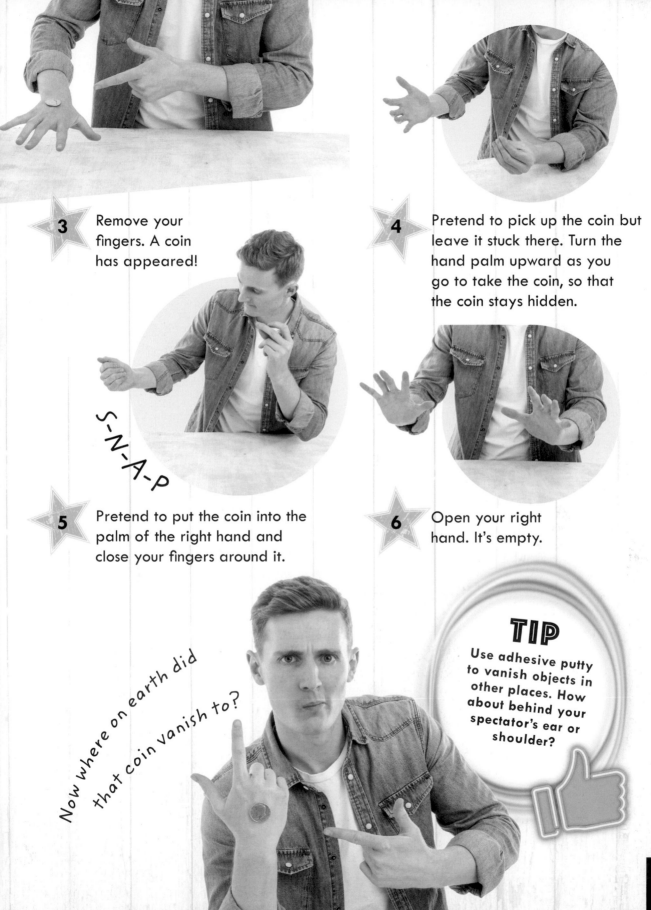

3 Remove your fingers. A coin has appeared!

4 Pretend to pick up the coin but leave it stuck there. Turn the hand palm upward as you go to take the coin, so that the coin stays hidden.

S-N-A-P

5 Pretend to put the coin into the palm of the right hand and close your fingers around it.

6 Open your right hand. It's empty.

Now where on earth did that coin vanish to?

TIP

Use adhesive putty to vanish objects in other places. How about behind your spectator's ear or shoulder?

MAGICAL COIN MATRIX

In this sneaky trick, you'll magically teleport four coins to the same place. You don't have to use a mat, but it will help to MUFFLE any telltale sounds.

KEY:

The path the coin SEEMS to jump.

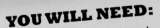

YOU WILL NEED:
- four coins • four playing cards • mat (optional)

1 Place the coins at the corners of the mat. Hold the cards in your left hand.

magician's view

2 Use your right fingers to slide the top card onto the first coin. At the same time, sneakily pick up the coin with your left fingertips.

3 Cover the second and third coins by sliding off the top card with your right fingers. Pass the last card (and hidden coin) to your right hand.

4 Casually show the face of the last card, hiding the coin under your fingers. At the same time, lift the top left card (as you view them) to reveal the coin underneath.

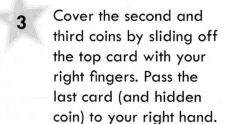

5 Lower the last card onto the fourth coin, and drop the hidden coin too. At the same time, lift the top left card, secretly picking up the coin.

magician's view

6 Discard the playing card in the right hand. Move the card with the hidden coin from the left hand to the right.

7 Lift the bottom left card and its coin with your left hand and place them on the three coins on the bottom right.

8 Turn over the last two cards. All four coins are in the bottom right. Magic!

TORN BANKNOTE ...RESTORED!

Rip a **GAPING** hole through the middle of a folded banknote...then unfold the note to show that it is still in one piece! Practice on a banknote-sized piece of paper first!

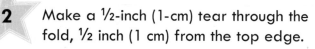

YOU WILL NEED:
- one banknote

1 Fold down the top quarter of the banknote.

2 Make a ½-inch (1-cm) tear through the fold, ½ inch (1 cm) from the top edge.

3 Fold the torn piece behind the back of the note, as you pretend to tear it off completely.

R-I-I-P-P-P!!!

magician's view

TIP
Scrape the banknote with your fingernail to make a ripping sound as your hand moves away.

4 Pretend to hold the torn piece in your fingers...then pop it into your mouth. Chew the imaginary piece of paper thoughtfully.

5 Grab the ends of the note, with the "V" toward you. Pretend to spit the piece of paper at it. At the same time, pull the ends of the banknote. It will appear to be magically restored. It will have a tiny tear, but your audience won't notice this!

TIP
Use a slightly crumpled banknote. That way, the tear will be even less visible!

49

BOBO'S COIN TRICK

This trick comes from one of the all-time greats of coin magic—JB Bobo. You just need a couple of different coins that the audience knows about, and a secret SPARE for the sleight of hand.

YOU WILL NEED:

- three coins, two the same (e.g. a dime and two pennies)

1 **Finger palm** a penny in your left hand, and have the other coins in your right fist. Say the two coins in your right hand add up to 11 cents —can your volunteer guess which coins they are?

2 Ask your volunteer to hold out their hand as you open your fist to reveal the dime and penny.

TIP

Even an easy question like this keeps your audience's minds occupied—leaving you free to perform sleight of hand!

3 Lift up the dime with the first finger and thumb of your left hand.

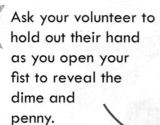

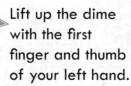

4 Go to toss the dime back onto your right palm, but actually release the finger-palmed penny by extending your left fingers. At the same time, pull down your left thumb and first finger to place the dime into finger palm.

SWITCHEROO!

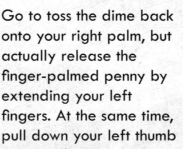

5 As soon as the extra penny lands and clinks against the other one, close your right fist.

6 Place the two pennies in the volunteer's hand. Use your fingers to cover them and your thumb to close up their fist, so the volunteer doesn't see the coins.

TIP
Ask your volunteer to pull out the dime or penny—it'll make them more sure that they are holding two different coins.

7 Ask the volunteer to pull out either coin without looking and place it on the back of their closed fist. Of course, they can only pull out a penny.

8 Pick up the penny. Toss it into your open right hand once, twice...and then on the third drop switch it with the dime (see step 4).

SWITCHEROO!

9 Pick up the dime with your left hand as you also finger palm the penny in that hand. Tell your volunteer to open their hand and they will find ...the penny!

The coins have magically switched places!

MUFFI SU ISE

This isn't the easiest of tricks but it's worth the effort for the **DELICIOUS** results. You just need to have the self control not to gobble up the main prop!

> **YOU WILL NEED:**
> • a muffin • cling wrap
> • two rubber bands • a knife
> • one coin • a permanent pen

> **!**
> **CAUTION**
> Ask an adult to help or supervise when you are cutting the muffin.

1 Wrap the muffin in cling wrap and secure with the rubber bands. Make a slit from the bottom of the muffin to about halfway up, cutting through the cling wrap.

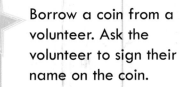

2 Borrow a coin from a volunteer. Ask the volunteer to sign their name on the coin.

3 Make some small talk about the muffin while you **false transfer** the coin from your right hand into your left.

4 Take the pen back with your left hand (the one secretly holding the coin) and tap it on your right hand.

5 Now open your right hand.

WHOA! WHERE'S THE COIN?

6 Pick up the muffin with your left hand and secretly push in the palmed coin. Start unwrapping the cling wrap.

magician's view

TIP
Hold the bottom of the muffin during the reveal so no one spots the slit.

7 Have your volunteer break off the top of the muffin to find their signed coin inside!

COIN TRICKS

MISER'S DREAM

Don't attempt this trick until you are really comfortable with coin magic. It's difficult —but it's also SPECTACULAR! You can make coins repeatedly appear from thin air!

YOU WILL NEED:

- two of the same coin
- credit card

1 Start with one coin in a **classic palm** in the right hand, the other **finger palmed** in your left, and the credit card in your right pants pocket.

2 Produce the finger-palmed coin from thin air! (Read about coin reproduction on page 39.)

3 Grab this coin with your right fingertips as you secretly release the classic-palmed coin from the right hand into the left.

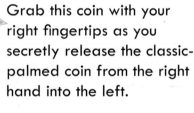

magician's view

4 Pretend to put the coin in your pocket. As your right hand goes in, push the coin back into classic palm. Bring out your hand, keeping the coin hidden and your arm relaxed at your side.

5 Repeat the production of the coin from the left hand (step 2) and switching it for the classic palmed coin (step 3), but this time really do drop the coin from your right hand into your pocket.

6 Produce the finger-palmed coin in your left hand and do a **false transfer** into your right hand. Pretend to put the coin in your right hand into your pocket.

7 Palm the credit card as you bring your right hand out of your pocket.

8 Produce the coin from your left fingertips one more time, holding it ready for a **shuttle pass.**

TIP
Try to keep your movements really smooth and natural.

magician's view

9 As your left hand moves to toss the coin into your right hand, turn over your right hand to reveal the credit card and finger palm the coin as normal. This is called a shuttle pass.

TIP
With perfect timing, it'll look as if the coin magically changed into a credit card!

SPEND! SPEND! SPEND!

TRICKS WITH EVERYDAY OBJECTS

When you take an ordinary object and do something **EXTRAORDINARY** with it, the magical effect is incredibly strong. Every trick in this chapter uses everyday items from around the home.

JUGGLING!

Juggling is a great skill and it's a good way to fill awkward gaps in your show. You just need to practice, practice, practice!

No need for special juggling balls—use your props!

KARATE CLIP

This incredible **STUNT** trick involves a sneaky switcheroo! You'll toss a paper clip into the air, and then miraculously skewer it in midair with your index finger.

YOU WILL NEED:
• two paper clips

1 Bend one of the paper clips outward so it fits on the tip of your right first finger. Keep the clip hidden here until the finale of the trick.

2 Hold up a paper clip to your audience in your left hand. Toss it into the air and catch it a few times.

TIP

Curl in your fingers so the clip is out of sight.

Gotcha!

3 On the third toss, snatch it with your right hand. At the same time, extend your right first finger so the bent paper clip can be seen and hold it still.

57

22

EVERYDAY OBJECTS

APKIN HANDS

This is the perfect mealtime trick. The only prop you need is a paper napkin and one-to-one close-up magic is always a winner!

R-I-I-P-P-P!!!

1 Take a small napkin and tear it in half. Roll each piece into a tight ball.

magician's view

2 Pick up one ball and do a **false transfer** into your right hand. Pick up the other ball in your left hand (without revealing the palmed one).

TIP

Keep your left hand relaxed so no one suspects it is holding the first ball.

3 Pretend to place the ball that's in your left hand into your volunteer's open palm—but really transfer the palmed one as well! Ask them to close up their fist.

4 Fist-pump the volunteer with your right hand. Slowly open your fist to show that the ball has vanished.

BAM!

5 Ask the volunteer to open their hand. Surprise! They are holding both the napkin balls!

The audience thinks that you're holding one ball and the volunteer's holding the other. In reality, the volunteer is holding both.

23

T I LE-JOI TEᴅ A M

Baffle your audience with this cool BODY ILLUSION! You'll seem to twist your arm through 360 degrees, while your spectator only just manages 180!

YOU WILL NEED:
• your arm—and a volunteer's!

1 Ask your volunteer to kneel with their right-hand palm down on the ground, fingers pointing outward.

2 Ask the volunteer to twist their hand toward the right as far as they possibly can.

TIP
Try the movements yourself first so you can see how an arm can and cannot twist.

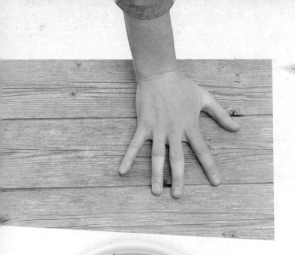

3 Copy the volunteer's actions until both your fingers face inward (180 degrees). Now lift your hand to point at the volunteer's wrist and say how tight it is now, and how they probably can't twist it much farther.

4 As the volunteer agrees, subtly replace your hand — but this time, you're going to twist it toward the left. Your hand seems in the same position as the volunteer's...

NO FARTHER

STILL TURNING

5 ...but now you can continue to twist your arm all the way back to the front. You might even be able to twist it farther than that if you're really supple!

24

LINKING RUBBER BANDS

Whenever you're using everyday objects, like these rubber bands, you can let your audience have a really close look at your props. They'll see there's **NOTHING** tricky about them and be even more impressed by your magic!

YOU WILL NEED:

• two rubber bands in contrasting colors, approx 6 in (15 cm) diameter

1 Hook the rubber bands round your first and third fingers as shown.

2 Use your thumbs to pull the bottom strand of the top band back and below the top strand of the lower band.

TIP

During steps 1 to 6, chat casually to your audience. Try to make it look as if you're just fiddling with the rubber bands.

3 Push your thumbs into this new space, use your second fingers to keep everything in place, then take out your thumbs.

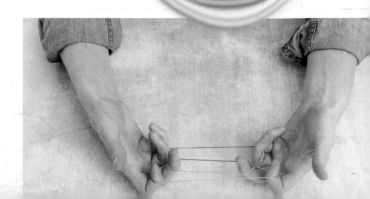

4 You are going to wrap the rubber bands around each other like this again. Take the second strand, which is part of the bottom band, and repeat the process with the third strand.

You've secretly intertwined the bands!

5 As your thumbs go into the new gap, pull out your second fingers. Once the bands have been twisted twice, put your second fingers back in.

6 Now close your fists. From the front it looks like you are just holding two rubber bands.

LINKED!

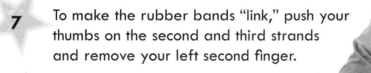

7 To make the rubber bands "link," push your thumbs on the second and third strands and remove your left second finger.

8 Now pinch the top band with your left hand and stretch the lower band, removing your right second finger. The bands will come apart!

TIP
If you loosen your pull on the top rubber band it'll dangle more freely—very convincing!

25

DOWN THE LADDER

Here's another simple but effective rubber band trick. Even though your volunteer is holding onto the banknote, it MYSTERIOUSLY moves down the different strands of band!

YOU WILL NEED:

• two rubber bands in the same color • one banknote

1 Ask a volunteer to fold the banknote in half lengthwise, then widthwise. Hold the rubber bands between your first and third fingers.

2 Push the top three strands back and behind the bottom strand with your thumbs.

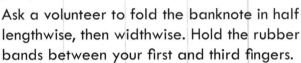
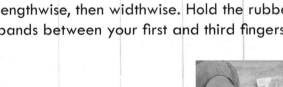

3 Hook your thumbs underneath and lift them back up so that all four strands separate.

4 Insert your third fingers into the bottom gap, your second fingers into the middle gap, and your first fingers into the top gap.

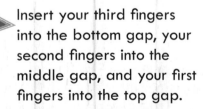

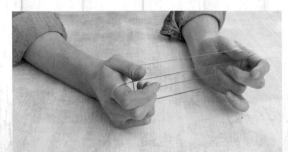

5 Close up your fists. From the front, it looks as though you are holding the rubber bands as normal.

6 Ask the volunteer to hook the banknote around the top strand.

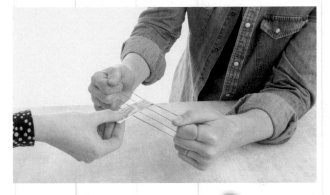

7 To make the magic happen, slip your first fingers out of the bands quickly. The top two strands will switch places and the note will move down a strand.

TIP

Magicians often use big movements to hide smaller ones. Move your hands grandly up and down and no one will notice you slipping out your fingers!

TIP

Make sure the rubber bands don't slip off your knuckles!

8 Repeat the same actions with your second and then your third fingers, for the note to move down all four strands!

26

NAPKIN ROSE

This isn't exactly a trick—it's more of a flourish...the perfect **FINALE** after a couple of close-up sleights of hand at the dinner table! You simply turn an ordinary paper napkin into a beautiful rose—but who will you give it to?!

YOU WILL NEED:

• one paper napkin

TIP

Most napkins are made of layers. Peel these apart and just use a single layer for your rose—it'll make the folds easier.

1 Loosely fold down the top third of the napkin. Now fold that part back upon itself.

2 From the top, carefully roll the napkin into a loose tube.

3 Pick up the tube and insert half of your first finger into the top. Pinch the napkin here and begin to twist with your other hand very tightly.

This will be the flowerhead!

4 Keep twisting down tightly until you get two-thirds of the way to the bottom.

This is the rose's stalk!

5 To make the leaf, pull up on the outside layer at the bottom and unfold it up onto itself.

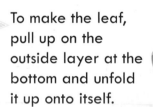

TIP

Pull gently so that you don't tear the thin napkin.

6 Below the leaf, pinch the napkin and use both hands to twist the rest of the stalk.

ROSES ARE RED, VIOLETS ARE BLUE, SUGAR IS SWEET...

27

TWO CORK TRICK

This trick is an absolute WINNER—and it's simple to master too. You just need to pay attention to how you position your fingers and thumbs.

YOU WILL NEED:

• two corks

TIP
The corks don't have to be the same.

1 Grip the corks between your thumbs and the base of your first fingers.

2 Twist your left hand toward yourself so your left thumb touches the bottom of the right cork and your right thumb touches the bottom of the left cork.

3 Now place your left first finger on the top end of the right cork. Reach your right first finger around and underneath your left thumb and place it on the top end of the left cork.

The part where your finger stretches around is the secret. When your audience try to copy this trick, they'll grip the corks in the most logical way—and won't be able to pull them apart!

BA-DA-BING!

4 Once all four ends of the corks are gripped, you will find that you can pull them apart.

5 To add finesse to the trick, half-twist your right hand as you move the corks apart. This'll make the corks perpendicular to each other—and convince your audience that you just pulled the corks through each other!

28

FUN Y FO K E D

This illusion is another classic! You start by bending a fork...or do you? With a little magic, the fork is soon back to normal. You can even take the trick further and create the illusion that the fork SNAPS!

YOU WILL NEED:
• one fork • a table

TIP
Before you begin, make a show of tapping the fork on the table so everyone can see it is real.

1 Grip the fork in your left hand so that your three middle fingers are over the handle and your little finger is under it. Push your thumb against the handle end and press the fork end against the table.

2 Create a bit of pressure by pushing down on the fork. This also reinforces the idea that the fork is solid.

! CAUTION
Check with an adult where it's okay to perform this trick. You don't want fork marks on their best table!

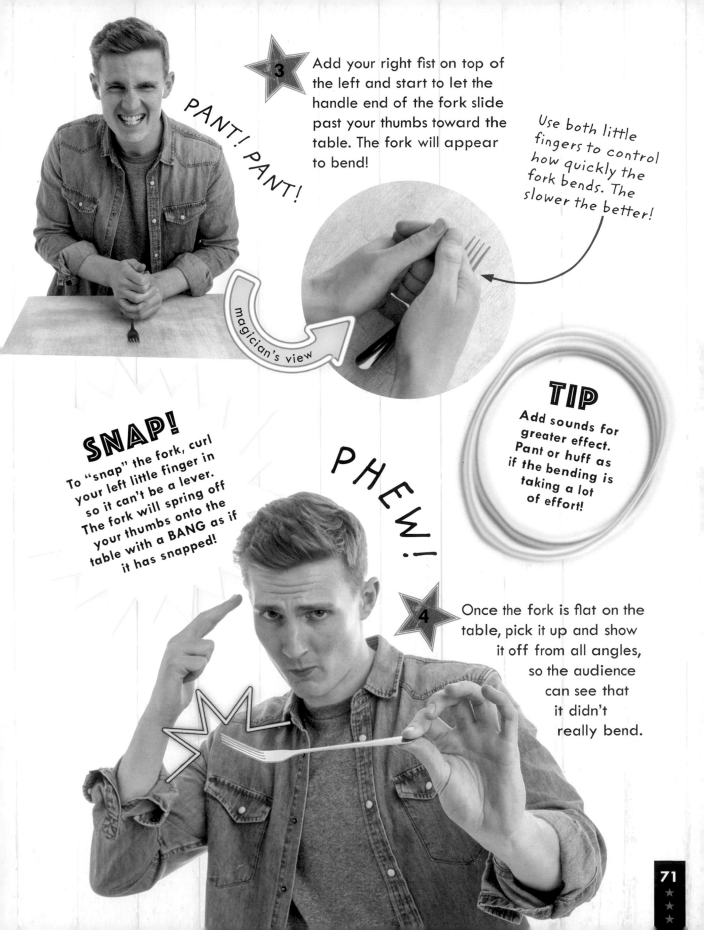

PANT! PANT!

3 Add your right fist on top of the left and start to let the handle end of the fork slide past your thumbs toward the table. The fork will appear to bend!

Use both little fingers to control how quickly the fork bends. The slower the better!

magician's view

TIP
Add sounds for greater effect. Pant or huff as if the bending is taking a lot of effort!

SNAP!
To "snap" the fork, curl your left little finger in so it can't be a lever. The fork will spring off your thumbs onto the table with a **BANG** as if it has snapped!

PHEW!

4 Once the fork is flat on the table, pick it up and show it off from all angles, so the audience can see that it didn't really bend.

29

SURPRISE DRINK

Talk about having tricks up your sleeve! For this illusion, you'll magically produce a glass full of orange juice from your jacket. All THRILLS and hopefully no spills.

YOU WILL NEED:
• tall glass • orange juice

To do this trick, you must be wearing jeans or pants that have a back pocket and you need to be wearing a long-sleeved jacket.

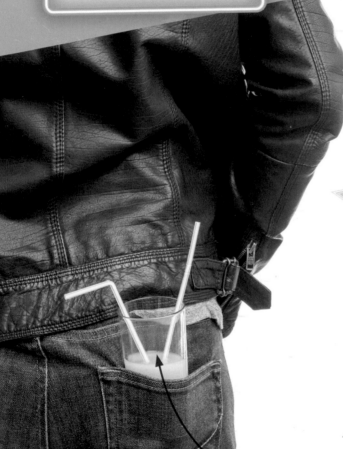

1 Before you begin your performance, half-fill the glass with juice and tuck it into your back pocket.

This trick is best performed onstage. Keep the glass out of sight until you magically produce it.

2 Greet your audience and start to take off your jacket. Shrug it from your shoulders and reach your right hand back to pull off the left sleeve, just as you normally would.

3 Once that sleeve is off, reach under your jacket with your right hand. Slowly and smoothly, start to pull the drink from your pocket. Let the jacket swing all the way around to the front, keeping your right hand and glass hidden behind it.

TIP
Make sure you have the left sleeve comfortably off and your right hand can grip the glass firmly before pulling it out from your pocket.

4 Let the jacket dangle as you pull the glass up through the sleeve, turning your sleeve inside out as you go.

5 Act surprised as you pull the glass out of the top of your sleeve.

SLURP!

MAGIC THREAD

Known to magicians as the Gypsy Thread Trick, this is an all-time classic. You tear a length of thread into pieces, and then MIRACULOUSLY restore them into one long piece again.

TIP

Make sure you use cotton thread for this trick. It's the easiest kind to break.

YOU WILL NEED:
• a spool of cotton thread
• a pencil

1 Unravel an arm's length of thread. Wind it around the end of a pencil, leaving 8 inches (20 cm) at the end.

2 Slide the wrapped-up thread off the pencil and scrunch it into a ball. Tuck it into the top of the spool with the loose end sticking out.

3 To start the trick, pull the loose end of thread and secretly pinch the little ball between your left thumb and first finger. Unravel about the same amount of thread from the spool as last time.

magician's view

4 Use your right hand to break the thread at the spool.

SNAP!

5 Break the thread into pieces around 6 inches (15 cm) long. Hold these in your left hand, where the secret ball is still hidden with its length of thread sticking out.

SNAP!

6 Pop all the loose pieces, except the one with the ball attached, in your right hand and roll them into a ball.

7 Now look as though you are going to stick the loose ball in your right hand to the last strand of thread in your left.

magician's view

8 As you push the loose ball into your pinched left thumb and first finger, let the prepared ball fall.

TIP
Gently blow on the thread for dramatic effect.

9 The original length of thread will unravel and it will look as though all the pieces are completely restored. Magic!

31

LINKING PAPER CLIPS

In this simple but effective trick, you'll make two paper clips FLY through the air like trapeze artists and end up magically linked. This is a great one for close-up magic.

TIP
Use bright, colorful clips that are easy to see.

YOU WILL NEED:
- one banknote
- two paper clips

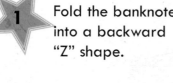
1 Fold the banknote into a backward "Z" shape.

2 Slide a paper clip over the first two layers at the top left-hand corner of the banknote, with the long side of the paper clip facing you.

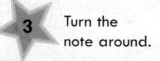
3 Turn the note around.

4 Slide the second paper clip on the same way, at the top left-hand corner of the banknote, with the long side of the paper clip facing you.

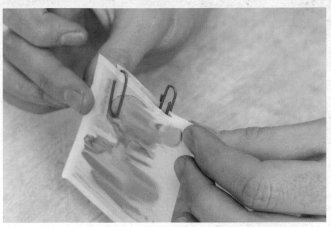

5 Pull each end of the banknote outward...

6 ...The paperclips will fly up and link in mid air.

TIP

Let your spectators examine the paper clips, so they can see that they are really linked!

CLIP!

32

STRAW TWIST

This is a great trick to keep friends and family entertained if you're waiting for food in a restaurant. You don't need ANY special props—just a couple of drinking straws and a volunteer.

YOU WILL NEED:
• two drinking straws

1 Hold the straws in a cross, with the vertical one below the horizontal one. Pull the bottom of the vertical straw up and over the horizontal one, take it to the left of its other end, and then fold it back down, so it's wrapped around once.

2 Ask your volunteer to hold on to the top and bottom ends of the vertical straw.

TIP

Holding the straw helps to convince the volunteer that you can't possibly be doing anything tricky.

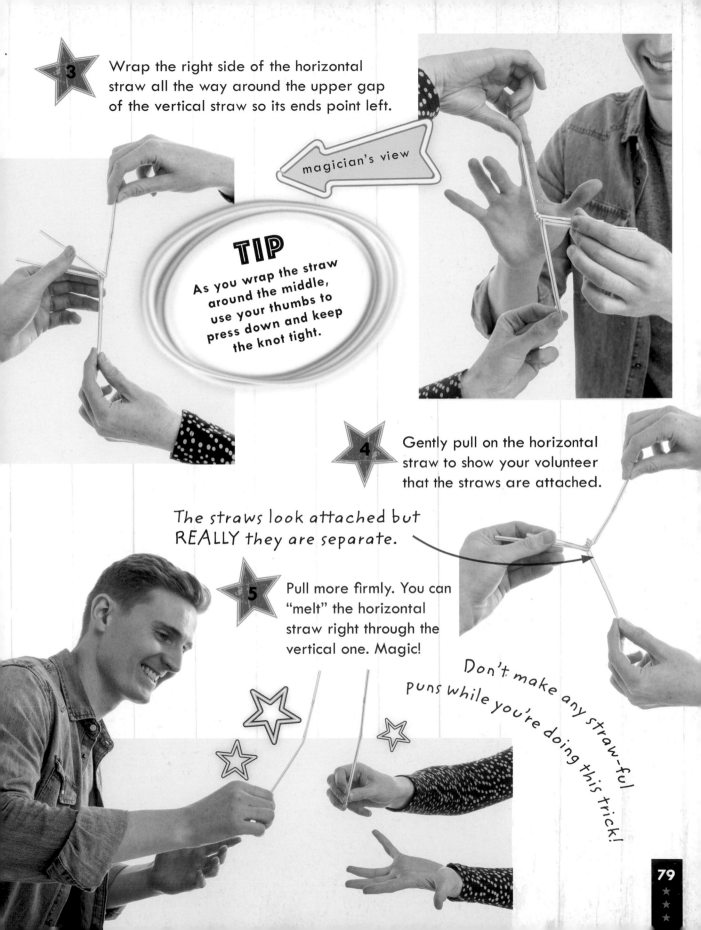

3 Wrap the right side of the horizontal straw all the way around the upper gap of the vertical straw so its ends point left.

magician's view

TIP

As you wrap the straw around the middle, use your thumbs to press down and keep the knot tight.

4 Gently pull on the horizontal straw to show your volunteer that the straws are attached.

The straws look attached but REALLY they are separate.

5 Pull more firmly. You can "melt" the horizontal straw right through the vertical one. Magic!

Don't make any straw-ful puns while you're doing this trick!

MOVING STRAW

How can you move a straw without touching or blowing it? There must be some explanation! Is it magic, magnetism, or some OTHER invisible force?

YOU WILL NEED:
- one drinking straw
- a small bottle

1 Before the trick, secretly rub the straw on your top—not too much or the straw will be too fast to control.

Rubbing the straw charges it with static electricity.

2 Balance the straw on the bottle.

TIP

Static electrical charge can be positive or negative. The same charges will push each other away. Opposites will attract.

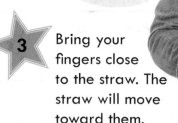

3 Bring your fingers close to the straw. The straw will move toward them.

Your fingers and the straw have opposite electrical charges, so they attract each other.

RISING RING

Magicians have a very grand name for an illusion where an object appears to rise into the air. They call it a **LEVITATION**. This method works with anything you can thread onto elastic—you don't need an actual ring.

YOU WILL NEED:
• a ring • a broken rubber band

TIP
Borrow a ring from someone in your audience—that way, everyone will know it's just an ordinary ring.

1 Thread the ring onto the piece of elastic, keeping the ring closer to one end.

2 Stretch out the rubber band.

magician's view

THE AMAZING, GRAVITY-DEFYING GOLD RING!

3 Lift your right hand up slightly so the band is being held at an angle. Keep about 2 inches (5 cm) of extra elastic hidden in your left hand.

4 Gently release the extra elastic through your pinched fingers and the ring will appear to rise up.

GUESS THE CANDY

Good things come in threes—but the trick here is that you appear to be using three candies, but really have FOUR.

TIP

Remember how we said that tricks are best performed in threes (see page 7)? This trick is a good one to perform in the middle of a trio.

YOU WILL NEED:

- four candies the same color

1 Start with one candy loosely **finger palmed** in your left hand and others on the table.

TIP

You could do this trick with pennies or marbles instead.

ONE...

2 Pick up one candy and toss it into your open right hand.

3 Pick up another candy. This time, as you toss it into your open right hand, drop in the finger-palmed candy too, and immediately close your fist.

TWO...

4 Pick up another candy. Appear to put this in your pocket, but finger palm it.

5 Ask the volunteer how many candies you have in your right hand. They should say "Two!" Reveal you have all three candies in your hand.

6 Repeat steps 1 to 5, but this time don't finger palm the candy at step 4—put it in your pocket. The volunteer may guess correctly this time, but that is okay. You're setting them up for the big finish.

7 Pick up one candy and **French drop** it, so it appears to go into your right hand but stays hidden in your left.

8 Close your right fingers. Pick up the last two candies with your left hand, keeping the third one hidden, and put all three in your pocket.

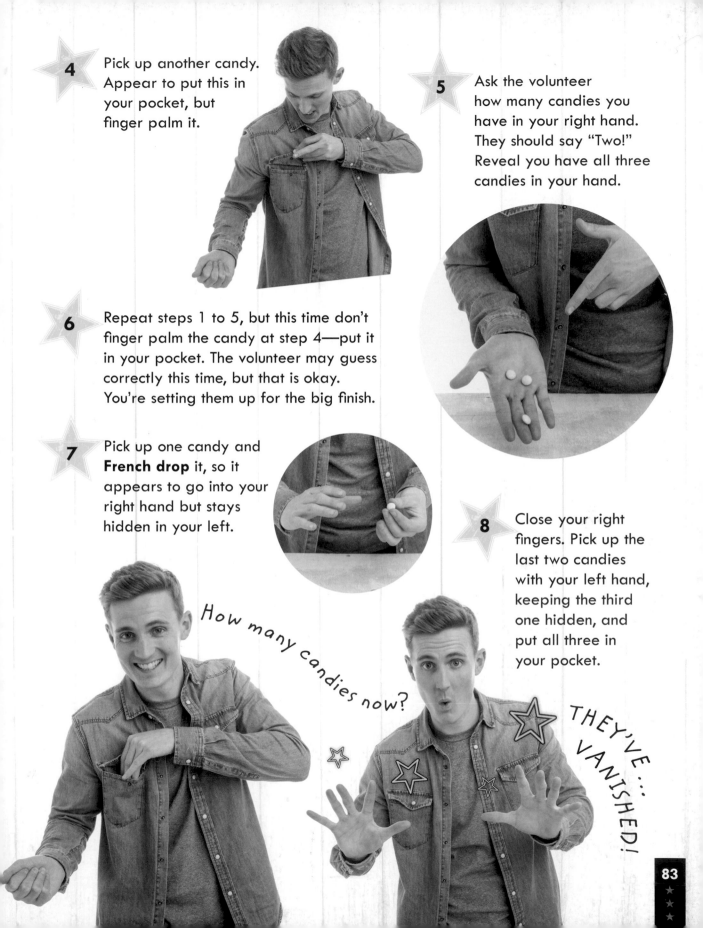

How many candies now?

THEY'VE... VANISHED!

36

CARROT CHOP!

In this trick, you'll turn into a magical NINJA, harnessing a secret force to chop a carrot in two with only a banknote. Just take care that no one can point the finger at you for cheating!

YOU WILL NEED:

• one banknote • a thin whole carrot or carrot stick

TIP

Borrow the banknote from someone in the audience—then everyone will know there's nothing fishy about it.

1 Fold the banknote in half lengthwise, making a big show of getting the crease nice and sharp.

TIP

Ask the volunteer to hold on tightly or the carrot will fall.

2 Ask your volunteer to hold out the carrot between their hands. Slice the banknote down onto the carrot ...of course, nothing will happen!

3 Do the same again. The first two attempts are just to build drama, and to prove to the audience that nothing tricky's going on (even though it will be).

magician's view

4 On the third try, extend your index finger along the edge of the note. If you strike it down forcefully, your finger will break the carrot.

TIP
Curl your finger back in again quickly so it looks like the banknote really did slice the carrot.

CHOP!

37

OUT TO LUNCH

This pocket trick uses a simple gimmick to DISAPPEAR part of a drawing. In the original version, a spectator initialled a card that said "Out to lunch." Those words were replaced by a picture—but the initials stayed the same.

YOU WILL NEED:

- blank business cards • a pen
- a thick rubber band • scissors

1 Draw a table on half of one of the business cards. Cut another business card in half widthwise.

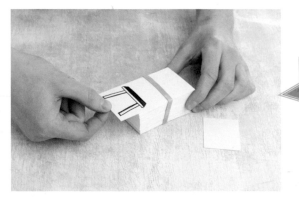

2 Place the drawn-on card on top of the stack and wrap the thick rubber band around the cards.

3 Place a blank half-card on top of the stack on the opposite side to the drawing.

TIP

Make sure the rubber band is thick enough to hold the blank half-card firm, even when your volunteer has the cards.

4 To perform the trick, ask a volunteer to draw something on the table.

How about a cute magic rabbit?

This is the underside and shouldn't be shown when you do the trick.

5 Turn the cards face down and pull out the whole card. The half card with the drawing will stay put because of the rubber band.

6 Place the card face down on the volunteer's hand, and pop the rest of the cards into your pocket. Do a magical wave or finger point...

7 Hey presto! The volunteer's part of the drawing has vanished.

THAT RABBIT'S HOPPED OFF!

CUP AND BALL

This fruity **GUESSING GAME** takes practice. Jake's version involves a lime and lemon, but you can just as easily use different colored balls or any other objects.

TIP
For this trick, you need to wear a jacket with two outside pockets.

YOU WILL NEED:

• one paper cup • one small ball • one lime • one lemon

1 Start with the lime in your left pocket, the lemon in your right pocket, and the ball in the cup.

Lemon in right pocket

Ball in cup

Lime in left pocket

2 Place your hand over the cup, turn it upside down, and pretend to take out the ball. Slide the cup onto the table. Pretend to place the ball in your left pocket, and grab the lime.

GAME 1...

3 Ask a volunteer if you took the ball or bluffed? The question will direct their attention away from the magic about to happen.

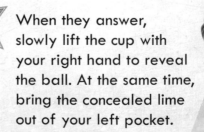

4 When they answer, slowly lift the cup with your right hand to reveal the ball. At the same time, bring the concealed lime out of your left pocket.

⭐ **5** Move the cup toward your body. Your audience is focusing on the little ball.

⭐ **6** Rest the cup on your left hand and sneak in the lime. Pick up the ball with your right hand and carefully put the cup back on the table.

TIP
Perform steps 4, 5, and 6 quickly and smoothly.

GAME 2...

⭐ **7** Use your right hand to put the ball into your right pocket. Ask your volunteer what's under the cup. Raise it to reveal the lime.

⭐ **8** Loosely palm the lemon in your right hand, bring the cup toward it, and pop it into the cup.

GAME 3...

⭐ **9** Pick up the lime with your right hand and rest it on top of the cup. Time for a final "What's under the cup?"—the audience will never guess it's a lemon!

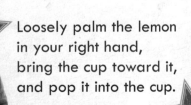

39

THE VANISHING BOTTLE

Trick your audience into thinking you're going to make a coin disappear...and then use misdirection to AMAZE them by pushing a bottle through a table instead.

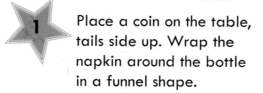

YOU WILL NEED:

- one coin • a small bottle or salt shaker
- one paper napkin • a table

1 Place a coin on the table, tails side up. Wrap the napkin around the bottle in a funnel shape.

2 Holding the bottle through the napkin, tap it on the coin a couple of times.

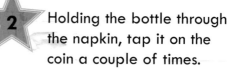

TIP

Tell the audience that the coin will disappear—it'll mean all eyes stay on the coin.

3 Move the napkin-wrapped bottle to the table edge. Suddenly "remember" the coin must be heads-up for the trick to work. This gives you enough **misdirection** to secretly drop the bottle from the napkin into your other hand and move it under the table.

4 Keep the napkin hand at the same height, as if it still contains the bottle, and move it back over the coin. The napkin should still hold the shape of the bottle.

TIP

Just as the bottle appears to pass through the table, tap the actual bottle on the underside of the table. This sound helps to sell the illusion.

5 Pretend to push the bottle right through the table, pushing the napkin till it's flat. Tell the audience that you've decided to make the bottle disappear instead of the coin!

For a finale, you could produce the bottle from under the table. Ta-dah!

40

FORK BALANCE

This BONKERS balancing act will leave your audience stunned. They won't know if you're using wires or magnets—but the answer is, neither!

> **YOU WILL NEED:**
> • two forks • a toothpick • a glass of orange juice • matches or a lighter (optional)

The prongs of the fork are called tines.

1 Loosely push the tines of the two forks together.

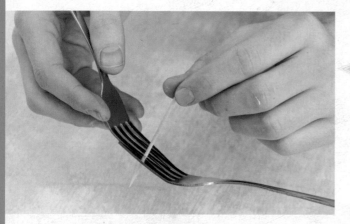

2 Push the toothpick through the middle point in the tines. You want about a third of it sticking out the other side.

3 Now push the fork tines together so that they are secure and the whole structure is stiff.

For step 5 you'll need a willing adult to help you.

4 Rest the toothpick on the edge of the glass so that the forks don't topple over. It takes practice to find it, but there is a perfect balancing point.

The forks stay balanced!

Thirsty work, magic!

5 Ask an adult to light the edge of the toothpick that is over the glass with a match or lighter. It will burn only as far as the inside edge of the cup. The forks will stay balanced.

MIND READING BASICS

From seeing something disappear or hearing an "impossible" prediction, ALL magic is a trick of the mind. Once you know the methods, mind reading is relatively simple, but your audience will find it jaw-dropping.

Mind reading often involves powers of memory. Flex your brain muscles with the exercise on the right, which will help you to remember random objects.

There are two main types of mind reading trick: those where you predict that something will happen; and those where you seem to pluck a thought from your spectator's mind.

MEMORY EXERCISE

Memorize this list—you'll notice each object rhymes with the number! Once you know it by heart, it can help you remember any list of 10 things.

In a show, ask volunteers to call out random objects. As each is called, try to create a picture in your mind that will link the object to its place on the list.

For example, if the first object called out is an elephant, picture an elephant biting into a huge sticky bun (because bun is number one on your special list that helps you memorize things).

1	Bun
2	Shoe
3	Tree
4	Door
5	Hive
6	Sticks
7	Heaven
8	Plate
9	Line
10	Hen

TIP
You can use this method to remember shopping lists or revision tips too.

You can even do this trick blindfolded.

If the second object is a window, imagine the window of a shoe shop—or better still, funny little windows on a shoe-shaped house.

The crazier and more visual the connection you make, the easier it will be to remember. With practice, you'll be able to memorize any list within about 20 seconds.

95
★
★
★

LOTTERY PREDICTION

Three spectators place nine numbered cards in three rows of three. The rows are completely random—so how come the magician can ALWAYS predict how much they total?

> **YOU WILL NEED:**
> • 11 index cards • a black felt-tip pen • an envelope • a piece of paper

1 Write 1665 on an index card and seal it in an envelope. You could also text the number to your volunteer. Just make sure they don't look at it until the end of the trick.

2 On nine of the other index cards, write the numbers 1 to 9. Arrange them into groups of three as shown here (left).

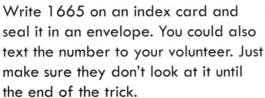

The mathematical secret to the trick is that each group of three adds up to 15.

3 Draw an arrow on the last index card.

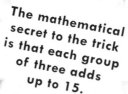

4 Stack each group on top of the other in any order. **False shuffle** the cards— pull off three cards, one at a time, and then dump the rest on top.

5 Choose three volunteers and hand each three cards.

6 Spin the arrow once to decide who goes first, then again to decide who goes second. In order, the volunteers place any one of their cards on the table.

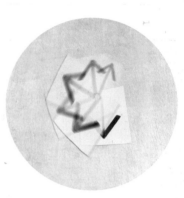

7 Ask the volunteers to put their second and third cards down in the same order. Now you have three, three-digit numbers.

8 Ask another volunteer to add up the total sum. They can use their phone calculator if they like. Then reveal your prediction.

The answer will always add up to 1665.

The total will be 1665!

CARD PEEK

A poker face comes in handy for this mind-blowing mind-reading trick. The only other things you'll need are a pack of cards—and the ability to take a SNEAKY peek.

1 Ask a volunteer to **shuffle** the cards.

2 Holding the deck face down in **biddle grip,** dribble the cards a few at a time from your right hand into your left.

TIP
Let the cards fall from your right thumb first, before releasing them from your right fingertips.

3 Ask your volunteer to call "Stop!" as you dribble the cards. When they do, show them the bottom card.

4 Put the two halves of the deck back together, keeping a **finger break** between them. Pass the deck to your volunteer for another shuffle—as you do, rotate your left-hand palm down so you can see into the gap between the two halves.

magician's view

5 Once you've seen the card, remove your finger from the break. Square the deck before you give it to the volunteer.

6 Pretend you don't already know the identity of the card. Add drama by asking if the card was black or red, high or low, odd or even...before you finally reveal their card.

TIP

What's the key to mind-reading tricks? You figure out the answer early on, and then act the part of sniffing out the answer. That way, people think that you've really read their mind.

CANDIES HAVE THE ANSWER

Wow your audience with this yummy elimination game. They'll never guess how you managed to predict which treat is left. SWEET!

YOU WILL NEED:
- a piece of paper • a pen
- a pack of colored candies
- four other chocolate bars

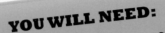

TIP
You could also send your spectator a text message with your prediction.

1 Beforehand, write "I knew you would choose the candies!" on some paper, roll it up, and put it in the pack of candies.

2 Place the pack on the table with the four chocolate bars.

3 Push forward any two except for the colored candies, and ask your volunteer to eliminate one.

The magic of this trick is that both you and your volunteer make choices—so they won't spot that you influenced the outcome.

4 It's the volunteer's turn. If they push forward the candies, don't choose them! Then you push forward two again (but not the candies).

5 You get to choose which of the final two to eliminate. Choose the one that's not the candies and then reveal your prediction. Amazing!

I knew you would choose the candies!

TIP
You can do this mind-reading trick for elimination games involving other objects —but you can't beat props you can eat.

DELICIOUS!

44

THIS, THAT, AND THE OTHER

This trick uses a principle of magic called **MAGICIAN'S CHOICE** or equivoque. You influence how the spectator views the outcome of their decisions to match your prediction.

YOU WILL NEED:
- three different objects (Jake used keys, a coin, and a lip balm) • cell phone

1 On the phone type a note:

You will have the keys, I'll have the coin, and the lip balm will be on the table.

TIP
It's more convincing if you type your prediction into the volunteer's phone, not your own.

TIP
Use any random objects for this trick—whatever your volunteer has in their pockets.

2 Place the objects on the table and ask the volunteer to point to two of them. Your next step depends which objects they pointed to...

a

b

c

Pick up both objects. Ask the volunteer to choose one of them.

Pick up the coin. Ask the spectator to point at one of the remaining objects.

Pick up the keys. Ask the spectator to point at one of the remaining objects.

3 For scenarios B and C, it doesn't matter which object the spectator chooses now. You are going to give them the keys or the coin, but never the lip balm (the lip balm must stay on the table for your prediction to be correct). This is the **magician's choice.**

If you prefer, use a pen and paper to write your prediction.

You will have the keys, I'll have the coin and the lip balm will be on the table.

4 Give them the choice to swap objects with you if they want.

5 If they are holding the key and you have the coin, ask THEM to read the prediction. If the objects are the other way around, read the prediction YOURSELF.

45

BOOK TEST

This is another mind-reading trick that relies on magician's choice. AMAZE your volunteer by knowing exactly which word they're thinking of.

TIP

Choose a funny or interesting force word to make your trick more entertaining.

YOU WILL NEED:

- two books, one with fewer than 500 pages and one with more

1 Beforehand, choose a page between 150 and 200 in the smaller book. Memorize the page number and the first word on the page (the **force** word).

2 Hold up the books. Ask the volunteer to point to one. Use **magician's choice** to give them the smaller book.

3 Tell the volunteer to say "Stop!" as you riffle through your book. Make sure you're close to the end when they do. Call out the page number, for example 672, and ask the volunteer to turn to that page in their book.

R-I-F-F-L-E!

R-I-F-F-L-E!

They can't! There aren't that many pages in their book.

4 Tell your volunteer that you'll try again but they must say "Stop!" sooner. This time, no matter what page you really open your book at, call out the number of the page you remembered.

5 Ask the volunteer to turn to that page, look at the first word on it, and imagine the word written in large letters in front of them.

TIP

For variety, try getting the word slightly wrong. For example, say "terrible" instead of "terrifying." It'll seem even more convincing!

6 Miraculously read their mind and reveal the word —letter by letter.

46

AN INSIDE JOB

This is a great trick for a magic show, as you'll need four volunteers. TANTALIZE them with the chance of choosing the envelope with money in it—they won't know it's just not possible.

TIP

The secret to this trick is that the money is never actually inside any of the envelopes.

1 Number the envelopes from 1 to 5 and fold the banknote.

magician's view

2 To perform the trick, fan the five envelopes and secretly hide the banknote behind them. Tell your audience that one of the envelopes contains a banknote.

3 Ask your first volunteer to choose an envelope. **Shuffle** the money away from that one, pull it from the spread, and give it to them.

4 Do the same with the other three volunteers. Each time, shuffle the money so it's still hidden. Finally, it will be behind the last remaining envelope.

magician's view

5 Ask each volunteer to look inside their envelope. They're all empty!

SURPRISE!

6 Slide your first finger into the last envelope. As you pull it out again, slide the money up from the back with your thumb. The banknote will look as if it came out of the envelope.

magician's view

THE MAGICIAN KEEPS THE MONEY EVERY TIME!

47

SALT PACKET PREDICTION

What are the chances of you always correctly predicting the last number in this elimination game? Actually, there's no CHANCE involved—just a little sneaky set-up.

YOU WILL NEED:

- eight salt packets
- cell phone

1 Beforehand, write the number 6 on the back of one of the salt packets.

TIP

You don't have to use a phone. You can just write your prediction on a piece of paper and fold it up.

2 Say you will send your volunteer a text message with your prediction but they must not read it. Text them the number 6.

3 Number the salt packets 1 to 8. Keep track of the secretly-prepared packet and make sure you write 6 on that one.

Now this one has 6 on both sides.

Whoosh!

★ **4** Ask your volunteer to gather up all the packets, then throw them onto the table.

★ **5** Tell them you will eliminate all the packets that don't have a number showing.

★ **6** Repeat until only the packet marked 6 remains. As it has a number on both sides, it can never be face down.

★ **7** Now ask the volunteer to read your prediction. BOOM! A game of chance becomes a miracle!

48

COLA CAN PREDICTION

Preparing the props for this trick takes patience—but you will certainly be rewarded. Watch your audience move from disappointment to DISBELIEF.

YOU WILL NEED:

• a cola can • a screwdriver • water • orange juice • reusable adhesive putty • a price sticker • a paper bag • a glass • eight index cards • a pen

CAUTION
Don't attempt this without adult help and supervision.

1 Pierce a hole near the top of the can with a screwdriver. Patiently pour out the cola, then rinse the can with water.

2 Using a straw, squeeze orange juice into the can up to the screwdriver hole.

3 Seal the hole with putty, then cover it with the "fake" price sticker. Pop the can into the bag.

4 Write a drink on each card. Mark the corner of the orange juice card on the back.

STILL WATER

ORANGE JUICE

FIZZY WATER

APPLE JUICE

MILK

COLA

TEA

LEMONADE

5 Place the bag and glass on the table, then hand out the cards to be **shuffled**. Now spread the cards face down. Locate the marked orange juice card and casually cut it to the top.

6 Ask your volunteer to choose a number from one to eight. Reverse-count cards from the top into your empty hand.

7 Show the bottom card and tell the volunteer to remember it. (This is a **force**.)

ORANGE JUICE

8 Say that the bag contains your prediction. Ask the volunteer to say their drink choice aloud. Bring out the cola can with a flourish.

AHHHH!

9 No worries. Open the can, pour the drink and—phew! —enjoy your applause. Liquid magic!

OOOOPS!

DRAWING DUPLICATION

In this mind-reading trick, you'll draw the same thing as your volunteer, without having seen their drawing. Is it STUPENDOUS mind-reading skill...or alphabet knowhow and a little sleight of hand?

TIP

Before the trick, order the cards alphabetically, with Apple at the top and Zebra at the bottom.

YOU WILL NEED:
• 26 index cards • two black felt-tip pens • two drawing pads

It's as easy as remembering the alphabet!

1 Write one word on each card as follows. Memorize the words.

APPLE	BOOK	CANDLE	DOG	EGG
FOOTBALL	GUITAR	HEART	INSECT	
JUG	KEY	LIGHT BULB		
NAIL	ORANGE	PENCIL	QUEEN	
RING	STRAW	TELEPHONE	UMBRELLA	
VAN	WRISTWATCH	XYLOPHONE	YACHT	ZEBRA

MUG

2 Spread the cards and ask your volunteer to choose one. As they do, casually **cut** the deck in half just as the spectator removes their card. You want to bring the card that was above the chosen card to the bottom of the pile.

3 Ask your volunteer to draw a picture of the word without letting you see.

magician's view

4 Pocket the cards, but secretly glimpse the bottom one. Whichever letter its word starts with, your volunteer's word will begin with the next letter. So if the card says "telephone," they must be drawing an umbrella.

5 Act as if you are reading your volunteer's mind while you do your own drawing.

6 Hold both pads facing your chest. Then, on the count of 3, turn them to face the audience. IT'S A DRAW!

ADD A SUM E

This trick is all about predicting the unpredictable—the answer to a sum involving three random numbers suggested by volunteers. So what's the SECRET? Predictably, it just takes a little preparation.

YOU WILL NEED:
- a notebook • a pen
- cell phone

1 On the first page of the notebook, write out a sum. Each line will have a three-digit number to add up—and each must seem to be in slightly different handwriting. Don't write the answer, though.

TIP
Alternatively, write your prediction on a piece of paper and place in a sealed envelope.

1759

2 Work out the sum in your head or with a phone calculator. Type the answer into your phone or text it.

3 Open the notebook on a page near the middle. Mark the three lines where your volunteers should write and add a line at the bottom. This should look just like your prepared sum, but without the numbers.

4 Hand out the notebook and ask three volunteers to each write a three-digit number next to one of the bullet points. Ask the last one to close the notebook.

TIP

The volunteer could use a phone calculator to add up the numbers.

5 As your volunteers return to their seats, give the notebook a magic flick. Now choose a fourth volunteer for the finale.

6 Open the notebook on the first page with your prepared sum. Ask the volunteer to write down the answer to the sum, and call out the answer.

7 Reveal that your prediction perfectly matches—and that you are a genius mind reader!

1759

MAGIC SQUARE

With some simple math and a good memory, you can create a magic number square on the fly for ANY random number between 50 and 100.

Yellow squares change each time you do the trick.

The numbers in the white squares always stay the same.

1 Memorize the following 4x4 number square.

11	6	? (3rd)	13
16	17+	7	10
5	12	14	? (2nd)
? (1st)	15	9	8

2 Ask a volunteer to pick any number between 50 and 100. Take 50 away from the number they choose to find your starting number. For example, if the chosen number is 60, your starting number is 10.

3 Fill in the first number of the magic square, the 17+ one. Add 17 to your starting number, 10. The number to write is 27.

4 In the first "?" square, put in the first number plus 1, so 28. Then in the second, plus another 1, so 29. And in the third, plus 1 again—30.

TIP

If you don't think you can remember where the numbers go, use a marker pen and stick on a secret cribsheet.

5 Fill in your memorized numbers as fast as you can. Hey presto! Every column, row, and diagonal adds up to the original number. Even the four corners and the four middle numbers add up to the chosen number too.

MIND-READING CODE

This clever code allows you to send thoughts to an accomplice—even if you are in different rooms! You start your sentences with special TRIGGER words, which each stand for a particular coin, number, or card.

YOU WILL NEED:
- a good memory
- an accomplice

 You and your accomplice must both learn and memorize the following code mastergrid:

The first seven trigger words all have the same number of letters as their corresponding number in the code.

WORD	COIN/CARD SUIT	NUMBER/CARD
I	Penny	1/Ace
OK	Nickel	2
CAN	Dime	3
WILL	Quarter	4
WOULD	Fifty cent	5
PLEASE	One dollar	6
PERHAPS	X	7
NOW	X	8
LET'S	X	9
SEE	Diamonds	10/0
HOW	Clubs	Jack
TRY	Hearts	Queen
COULD	Spades	King

HOW IT WORKS

With this code, you can secretly send information in sentences that sound perfectly ordinary. You start each sentence with a trigger word.

To secretly say what coin your volunteer is holding…

—If they are holding a fifty-cent coin, say to your accomplice:

"Would you be able to tell us what coin they are holding?"

"Would" corresponds to fifty cents on the code mastergrid (see left).

To secretly say the year date of the coin your volunteer is holding…

—If it was made in 2012, you need to send your friend the number "12"—but there is no code for that! So you use two sentences:

"I can see the date. OK, I'm going to give you just one chance to tell us what it is!"

"I" corresponds to 1 on the code mastergrid and "OK" corresponds to 2. So the year date is 12, meaning 2012.

To secretly indicate the card your volunteer is holding…

—Use two sentences—the first for the card and second for the suit. If you say:

"Could you tell us all the card? Try your hardest!"

The first "Could" corresponds to King on the code mastergrid. The "Try" corresponds to Hearts. So the card is the King of Hearts.

GLOSSARY

BIDDLE GRIP
An overhand grip that keeps control of the top cards (see p12).

CLASSIC PALM
Hide in the palm of the hand.

CUT
To split a deck of cards into two.

DOUBLE LIFT
Appearing to lift one card but lifting two.

FACE CARD
A playing card that is a king, queen, or jack.

FAKE TAKE
A way to make a coin vanish (see p39).

FALSE SHUFFLE
A way to appear to shuffle a deck of cards, but keep one or more cards in a particular order.

FALSE TRANSFER
A way to make a coin vanish (see p39).

FINGER BREAK
Using a finger to keep a gap between two parts of a deck of cards (see p12).

FINGER PALM
Hide in folded-over fingers.

FORCE
An object that a volunteer thinks they pick, but that is controlled by the magician.

FRENCH DROP
A way to make a coin vanish (see p38).

HINDU FORCE
A method to force a playing card on your volunteer (see p13).

KEY CARD PRINCIPLE
Knowing where the chosen card is in relation to a key card that the magician has already peeked at.

MAGICIAN'S CHOICE
When a magician forces an outcome, but makes it look like the volunteer has free choice.

MECHANIC'S GRIP
An underhand grip that allows you to deal and control the cards (see p12).

MISDIRECTION
To control the audience's attention.

SHUFFLE
To rearrange the order of the cards completely at random.

SHUTTLE PASS
A way of visually changing one object for another (see p55).

SUCKER TRICK
A deliberate mistake in a trick, made to make the finale even more impressive.

THUMB PALM
To conceal a coin at the base of your thumb.

TOP CARD CONTROL
A method to keep a chosen card at the top of the deck (see p13).